Golfing from the Right Side of the Brain™

How to Cure the Slice

By Dr. Bob Burton

Acknowledgements:

Thanks are due to some special folks.
To Mr. David Cline, whose keen observations as a
teacher of the golf swing made things happen. To Dr. Rick Yates,
who early on encouraged the writing of this book and then
provided much-needed feedback along the way.
Finally, to Catherine Harrison and Dr. Craig Harrison,
who revealed the pathway needed to publish my first book.

To my son, Sam, who asked the right questions,
this book is lovingly dedicated.

Table of Contents

About the Author

D r. Robert Burton was not always a golf fanatic. But pretty close to it. A golfer from a young age, he was born and raised in Winnsboro, Texas where the only greens are in the pastures around springtime. Nevertheless, he persevered in his pursuit of better golf courses and higher education, attending The University of Texas at Austin where he received his Bachelor of Arts degree in zoology in 1969.

A true Texan at heart, he went on to receive a Bachelor of Science degree in Health Care Science from The University of Texas Health Science Center in Dallas and a Master of Arts degree in vertebrate physiology at The University of Texas in Austin.

He attended The University of Texas Medical Branch in Galveston, Texas, and after long hours, late-night shifts and too many exams, he received his medical degree in May of 1985. He then did an internship in internal medicine at Baylor Hospital in Dallas, Texas, and following that, packed his winter duds and moved to Minnesota to serve as a resident at The Mayo Clinic.

He is the real deal—board-certified by The American Board of Psychiatry and Neurology. He completed a fellowship in the specialty of electrophysiology, consisting of the study of electroencephalography (that's four e's) and epilepsy surgery at The University of Texas Health Science Center in Houston in conjunction with Hermann Hospital. He is married to a very understanding and longsuffering wife, Lisa, who has accompanied him on his journey back from being a golf addict and has two wonderful children, Sam and Ellen.

Introduction

I would like to set the record straight once and for all.

When it comes to golf, it's a "brain thing." I do not mean a psychological brain thing. I mean a neurological brain thing. Now don't misunderstand me. You don't have to become a neurologist or a neurosurgeon to play golf. But as a practicing neurologist, I think the brain is grossly underrated as to its importance and relevance in the game.

My purpose in writing this book is not to confuse readers with a lot of medical mumbo-jumbo about the brain. Although I *could* bore you with a fantastic lecture on neuro-circuitry, if you like. Likewise, I do not pretend to be a great teacher of the swing or the game itself.

On the other hand, I do feel that some knowledge about the brain, and the nervous system itself, may make for better golf. It may not make medical history. But it makes sense. It has worked for me. But before you run out and hire a sports neurologist or fire your sports psychologist, let me introduce you to a few key points concerning my idea. I promise to hold back on the neuro-circuitry lecture until later.

Chapter One

Golf Is a Brain Thing

First things first. There are two sides to the brain. There is a left side and a right side. Pretty simple, huh? At first glance, these two sides may seem very similar in a generic sort of way. However, this is not entirely true. Every golfer, every person for that matter, has a dominant side or half of the brain called the dominant hemisphere. The side that develops as the dominant hemisphere manifests itself early on and is permanently in place by the time a child is a toddler or around three to four years of age.

What are these "dominant" features? For the most part, they are "motor" and "language" centers. And most of us are created with this dominance on the left side of the brain. But whoa! Aren't most people right handed? Exactly. However, the brain information for the right side of the body starts out in the left hemisphere. It's kind of a criss-cross of information coming from the left side of the brain to direct the right side of the body. It's not by accident that there are so many right handed clubs on display in your local Edwin Watts store. It's a calculated inventory based on the high percentage of right handed golfers.

By now you may have uttered your first, "So what?" and wondered what this has to do with golf anyway. Well, consider this. Dominance means just that. The left side of the brain seemingly plays a domineering role. And, as you may already know, where there is dominance, submission follows closely behind.

Now get this, the majority of golfers (80-90%) have a significant "flaw" in their golf swing, and approximately 90% of golfers are naturally right handed. Interesting statistics, huh? Furthermore, this fatal flaw is frequently a slice, defined as a type of shot where the ball curves dramatically from left-to-right for a right handed player, or right-to-left for a left handed player. And we don't have to look very far to begin to understand a potential problem in this regard.

I propose that the reason for this very common problem is related to brain dominance. Furthermore, one can even go a step further and ask if the problem in the swing is related to the fact that most of us are placing our stronger, dominant side away from the target. As a result, we are setting up a situation where the right arm and shoulder demand outright control in the swing...no matter the consequences. And that, my friend, begets a big ol' "slice" of brain dominance.

A Southpaw Switch

Let me cite a personal experience to further illustrate my point. My father taught me to play golf when I was about 12 or 13 years old. By that time, I was entrenched in complete right hand dominance. That is, I wrote with the right hand, batted and threw a baseball with the right hand and even had right eye dominance. My dad, on the other hand, was left handed. A lefty. Southpaw. Whatever you want to call it, he had beautiful handwriting and managed to avoid awkward positions many left handers get into when writing a composition.

He also played baseball and even pitched, all as a southpaw. His golf swing, however, was from the right side. Like so many challenges left handers face swimming upstream in a right handed world, he felt this departure was encouraged and even necessitated by his golf teacher's ultimatum. "You won't be able to get equipment of the same caliber or quantity, Fred, unless you swing from the right side," his teacher had warned.

Being in his early 20s, the idea of facing a future bereft of quality golf motivated him to make a conscious decision to swing from the right side. Guess what? He became a scratch golfer fairly quickly. He always hit the ball with a relatively medium altitude and a slow draw. I never saw him slice the ball. On weekends, we would load our clubs into Dad's 1949 Plymouth, which was always our second car, and drive to one of East Texas' many nine-hole golf courses. There, I mastered the skills necessary to being a weekend golfer. But ironically, unlike what you might expect, these frequent games did not bring my father and me closer together...not on the course, anyway. While he masterfully picked a spot just to the left of center and delivered each shot accurately, I was busy honing a natural out-to-end swing that placed me squarely in the nearby piney woods, always situated to the right.

The ever optimist, I rationalized that if I went out of bounds and/or lost the ball, I got to hit a second tee-shot. I was always amazed that Dad could hit the ball so well while I, being bone of his bone, flesh of his flesh, struggled mightily to no avail. At the time, I simply believed that the good golf swing gene had skipped a generation, and I was stuck with a defective swing.

Again, you might offer your condolences regarding my plight but still politely ask, "So what?" Consider this. After my training as a neurologist and some experiences in private practice, I began to think about the fact that left handers like my dad frequently have mixed dominance when it comes to brain development. In other words, they are seemingly able to "switch" to the right side more easily for specific tasks. Not so with right handers who have very little variation in that regard. This information, coupled with my own suspicion that placing the dominant side toward the target might be an advantage, led me to rethink my fatalistic theory about my ailing golf swing.

Soon, the evidence for my theory began to snowball. My dad was a frequent tennis player with a mean backhand like the rest of his family. As a result, his golf swing really translated to a left hander's backhand. A-ha! Not only that, he was an outstanding switch-hitter in baseball.

Still not convinced? What if I were to tell you Ben Hogan, Johnny Miller, Nick Price and maybe even Tiger Woods have been said to be left handed? You won't read that in *Golf Digest*. But the real question for us right handers is whether the vast majority of golfers errantly swing from outside-in because of an overriding dominance of the right side of the body which opposes the target.

You've Lost That Lovin' Feeling

I often dreamt of the pleasure it must be to be able to strike a ball that sails effortlessly 250 yards down the fairway with a nice draw at the end but never experienced it. I was all too familiar with the discommodious sensation of producing a banana ball. And the only birdies I was familiar with were in the trees, not in the game. Golf was not exactly my friend.

In contrast, my father always seemed to be happy on the golf course. Many of my friends profess to "think of nothing else" and be able to "forget" all their troubles when they play golf. I believe this phenomenon has some validity beyond the euphoric feeling of being free from the office, cell phone and computer. Could it be that these people have somehow gotten in touch with the usually submissive, non-dominant side of the brain? It is certainly a possibility since the non-dominant right brain contains pleasure and emotional centers that can be verified with electrical stimulation intraoperatively.

Likewise, these same centers often seem to be obliterated in those patients who have sustained strokes in the same non-dominant side of the brain. They often appear to be in a saddened and depressed state far beyond the expected grief of a sudden life change. Tiger Woods has, in so many words, described himself as somewhat shy, and yet he implies the golf course affords him a sense of well-being and a certain amount of comfort. How wonderful if each of us experienced the benefit of golfing from the non-dominant side of the brain—that pleasure-centered storehouse! Coupled with new information about perception, position and motor function of the non-dominant left side of the swing, I began to realize that success was more attainable than I once thought. If others could get in touch with the right side of the brain, then why couldn't I? Perhaps this approach was the alternative I needed.

Enter *Golfing from the Right Side of the Brain.* My purpose in writing this book was to find a suitable approach to correcting or even eventually curing the major swing flaws that were manifestations of brain dominance, based on my experiences as a neurologist and a longtime, frustrated golfer. Realizing the majority of us adult right handers can never physically change our swing orientation, (although one can imagine the chaos at Edwin Watts if we could) I have come up with a solution that works for me—both mentally and physically. Are you ready to find out more about the benefits of how to golf from the right side of your brain? Well, read on!

Chapter Two

Ball Flight F(Laws)

So what's the problem? After all, the game of golf is ancient, and barring the possibility that ancient golfers were actually super-intelligent aliens who happened to land their spaceship in Scotland, there shouldn't be so much difficulty with the swing for us earthlings. Which leads to the question, "Has this always been the case, or is this a more recent modern phenomenon?"

In other words, is it truly a brain problem or not? Certainly, our professional teachers are aware of the ball flight laws. In short, the ball-flight laws focus on the flight of the golf ball, based on two major factors: the path of the downswing and the position of the club head at impact. I suspect that most teachers of the swing who understand the concept of the ball-flight laws as an established teaching are aware that most golfers swing with a swing plane from outside to in, resulting in an ineffective but consistent slice.

But let's suppose for the sake of argument (and in order for me to have a successful book) that the problem does originate in the brain. Then the standard teaching lessons may be 30 minutes of wasted time and money unless your pro is aware of this fact.

On rare occasions, I have taken a golf lesson with a PGA teaching pro at a local country club. On one such occasion, after an arousing period of out-to-end swinging, my club pro made an astonishing observation. He revealed to me that I was not "finishing my swing." I was puzzled by the phrase but became intrigued nonetheless. After a few more swings with much effort, I finally admitted I did not fully understand what he meant. He then went on to say that he thought the problem could be helped, but he felt it was largely "psychological."

I stared at him in disbelief. Surely he was simply over zealous to make the latest hot topic available to the membership. Perhaps he had just read the first edition of *Tin Cup* (the movie had not come out at that time). For some reason I continued to take this suggestion very hard. I was astonished that a teaching professional felt my swing flaw could be the result of a glitch in my psyche. After all, I was a physician for Pete's sake! Not only that, I was a neurologist with a board certification by the American Board of Psychiatry and Neurology. How could this happen to me of all people?

I began to casually inquire whether other members had been told of any golf-related psychological hang-ups. I discovered much to my dismay that I was the only one! Initially, I panicked. Then I decided to do the only reasonable thing a man could do.

I would simply suppress this information forever.

However, I was not prepared for what happened next. My swing got worse. Worse! Every effort I made only resulted in more flaws piled atop of an already unsound swing. Fortunately, I resisted spending a bundle of money on sessions with a sports psychologist getting to know my inner golfer. However, I kept hacking away, albeit with an increased sensitivity to my mood and what I was "feeling" during the swing. I even tried swinging in tempo to the psychological mantra, "I'm okay (takeaway). You're okay (downswing)." On one occasion I developed a panic attack on the easiest hole on the course. Everyone at the clubhouse was talking about it, and I became even more desperate.

I realized I was not okay.

What's in *Your* Wallet?

At that point, I began to accelerate my spending. In one year, I purchased several complete sets of clubs in the attempt to buy a swing with no-fail equipment. I was an equipment manufacturer's dream. Perhaps a little offset in the irons and woods, coupled with a lighter-than-air shaft, superimposed on titanium inserts, with a Greg Norman Secret thrown in for good measure. Technology was the answer!

I would dash out to the course and blast away armed with my pristine clubs and my latest swing gimmicks. I wisely chose to ride the course on a cart, conserving all my energy so I could devote it to the fabulous swing awaiting me at the next hole.

What I was, in fact, doing was spending hours on the range perfecting my flawed swing. My wife shared my frustration, albeit she was more disturbed by the obvious change in my personality. Admittedly, I was not always clear-headed in my selections of the latest and greatest technology and did face some pretty valid criticisms from her regarding my spending habits. Especially the time I proudly toted home a new set of irons, like a hunter having bagged his prey, only to discover I had already stored an identical set in my garage.

When I trudged through the front door a little late from a day at the range one day, she sarcastically commented, "Are you going to rent a room at the golf range?" This admonition went unanswered as I robotically went out to the garage where I proceeded to clean my new $500 driver/combination ball retriever and re-organize my ever-growing collection of clubs.

One day after arriving home from a very trying day at the office, I spotted a collage of sorts as I turned into the driveway. At first, I thought the neighbors' kids had pulled out every toy from the garage and carelessly forgotten to put them away after a day's play. As I eased the car up closer, I suddenly recognized whose toys they were. Mine! My wife had mightily heaved each golf club from its revered place in the garage and scattered them all over the yard. I cried as I spent the next hour tenderly picking them up one by one. I went to bed early and alone for the first time in our marriage.

"You Ain't Got One"

Just when I thought that my family, my career and my happiness would be destroyed by a ridiculous game, I came to a new and much needed conclusion. One night, while dutifully watching an instructional program on the Golf Channel, I heard a teaching pro named Arnie Frankel talking about past experiences with his students. He recalled a student asking him to tell him what the problem was with his swing. To which Arnie dryly replied, "You ain't got one."

I suddenly awoke from my late-night fog. Arnie was talking about me! Over the years, I had foolishly spent several thousand dollars on equipment in hopes of salvaging a swing I did not possess. It was at that moment that I realized I indeed had a psychological problem.

I was suffering from addiction.

Nothing you could go to jail for or anything. I had simply become a victim of golf retailers from Dallas to Houston and all points in between. A true believer, I thought golf success was for the taking as long as one had the right equipment technology. But I had been had. Upon realizing my foolishness, hope vanished, the struggle subsided, and like John Daly in a dry county, I breathed a sigh of relief. It was decided. I would quit playing the game I loved but could never love me back.

Chapter Three

Get a Grip Man!!

I functioned fairly well in the beginning. Occasionally, a golf thought would traipse through my mind, and I would quickly try to ignore it. However, I did allow myself to ponder at times, "Was this ever a learnable game? The ancestors of golf surely must have had some comment about this." As far as I was concerned, playing golf "correctly" was impossible, at least for modern day golfers.

Then the event that I really needed came my way. After medical school, an internship, my residency and a few years in private practice in neurology, I was invited to do a year of training in epilepsy surgery. Interviewing for the fellowship position was a very pleasant conversation regarding my credentials, experience, the usual stuff. Then something wonderful and unexpected happened. The person who was to become my mentor in EEG (brain-wave analysis) and epilepsy asked me what I did in my spare time for fun. I quickly plucked my old standby for the section on hobbies and related to him that I was a golfer. At that point, his eyes brightened, he smiled a knowing smile, and for the next 30 minutes we talked about his favorite hobby—you guessed it, golf. To this day, he and I joke that was the only reason I got the fellowship.

A Chance to Heal

It was during this period that I learned a lot more firsthand about the phenomenon of brain dominance while mapping out extremely important functional areas of the brain. These areas included centers located on the surface of either side of the brain that controlled voluntary motor function of the corresponding opposite side of the body.

Knowing the exact location of these important "cortical" functions allowed us to more effectively monitor and predict the potential risk and benefit of doing something previously unimaginable in neurological surgery. We could safely remove damaged or abnormal brain tissue where electrical "chaos" was causing frequent seizures in epileptic patients. It was as though these renegade nerve cells had somehow gained control, and they were literally dominating the waking and sometimes even the sleeping hours of the patient's brain.

I spent much time analyzing and evaluating reams of paper containing recorded brain activity with both normal and abnormal electrical waves. Coupled with brain scans and a psychological profile of the patient, we could determine if surgery was a viable option. If so, we scheduled a WADA test, where a catheter was placed into a major artery in the leg, allowing it to "float" up to the heart and subsequently lodge into the various branches going up to the brain.

We then took X-Rays using dye to record the anatomy of the brain blood flow—critical evidence the neurosurgeon would need to remove the abnormal brain tissue. However, of equal importance, was the topic you and I have been discussing so far—brain dominance.

While it is true that at least 90% of right handers also have their language center on the left, one must be certain prior to operation. While the patient was awake, we determined "language dominance" by the injection of certain drugs to literally render this area nonfocusing for a short period of time. We injected a special chemical directed to the left side of the brain and then the right side that actually caused language function to temporarily cease, notifying us which side held the language center.

I also began to learn and appreciate the fact that the various parts of the brain communicated with each other, and a myriad of pathways existed to allow one part of the brain to "talk" to another (see the Appendix for a representation). This was a new dimension of my appreciation for dominance, and I realized what an appropriate descriptive term it was.

The dominant left side of the brain was charged with processing verbal data and then somehow translating it to the non-dominant right side. Given the fact that our world is based on language and analytical data, I held the left side of the brain in almost exclusive esteem. However, later on I would balance out my appreciation of the two and give more credit to where credit was due—the under-utilized, unsung hero, the right side of the brain.

The Man with Two Brains

Occasionally, a different problem would surface. For example, one patient would have such frequent and violent seizures that he could not function in his daily life. Further study revealed that although the patient's seizures were coming from one area on one side of the brain, the seizure activity was spreading so fast across a deep connection to the other side of the brain that the patient would literally crash to the floor. We could not remove the abnormal area causing the seizure as we did in other patients because it would render him paralyzed. Likewise, no combination of medicine would help.

The surgeons decided to perform a radical surgery to *disconnect* the two sides of the brain and offer him the opportunity to improve his quality of life. Following the operation, the patient had a remarkable recovery with very few seizures. Likewise, medication then became of much greater benefit in preventing further seizures. The surgery was, however, not without some sacrifice on the part of the patient. For a significant period of time after the surgery, he experienced **disconnection syndrome**. The previous communication pathways between both halves were destroyed. The importance of the dominant side telling the non-dominant side of the brain what to do was never more clearly demonstrated. It was as though this patient had two brains existing in one body.

Fortunately, the man's brain adapted well with the passage of time, and it was a joy to see his return to normalcy. This experience of disconnection syndrome continued to add to my understanding of brain dominance and fuel my growing theory about its role in the golf swing. As a result of my studies and experience, the picture of "harmony" necessary between the two halves of the brain could not have been clearer. As you will appreciate later on in this book, these foundational realizations evolved into one significant conclusion having to do with my thesis—that is, golf is a brain thing!

Chapter Four

Lessons for Sam

A year after our marriage, we had a daughter, Ellen. Priorities became quite clear, and golf faded even farther from my mind. I was now back in private practice, and my only thoughts were about the preschool we would choose, the church we would attend and the safety record of my wife's new car. Equipment mattered only as long as it was a crib, high chair, playpen or stroller, and by the time my daughter was a year and three months old, my wife was pregnant again, and we were going to have a boy.

At that point, the "G" word was no longer even uttered, and I was walking on clouds. Just when I thought things could not possibly get any better, they did. It was a rainy day, and my wife and I were casually surfing through the TV channels and discussing potential names for our son. Admittedly, I was half-asleep, and my defenses were down. However, the name "Sam Sneed" wafted over the air waves and stirred me to consciousness. The CBS channel was broadcasting a feature on the upcoming Master's Tournament highlighting one of the greatest golfers, and my boyhood idol, Sam Sneed. Suddenly it hit me. "Sam would be a good name for our son," I offered hopefully. And another Sam was eventually born.

Our home welcomed Sam's new arrival with a great deal of fanfare and hoopla. It was pure excitement. Ironically, around the same time, a new name was emerging in the world, the likes of which had never been witnessed. His name was Tiger, and he burst onto the scene with unprecedented publicity approaching mythological proportions. He became a player at an age when most kids were still struggling to escape from diapers. At age 19, he was golf's demi-god.

My wife learned quickly that Tiger's mother was also Oriental like herself, and this gave her new thoughts about the potential for our new son. In fact, to my surprise, my wife became instantly interested in this golfing phenomenon. Feeling somewhat of a kinship with the mother of such a great golfer, she envisioned that our son could also be a great golfer. Sam, from that moment on, was destined for an early start in golf, and I was appointed to play the role of Earl Woods, a task to which I felt unequal. Of course, until such time that Sam was ready to play golf, I would beg off becoming involved again in the game.

Drawing on the Right Side of the Brain

One day my wife brought home a book from her drawing class at the local college. It was entitled, *Drawing on the Right Side of the Brain.* [1] Without really thinking about what I was saying, I casually tossed out the idea that I would like to write my own book someday about golfing from the right side of the brain. There again, as much as I tried to suppress my golfing habit, it arose with the least bit of prompting.

I awaited the first time Sam and I would venture out together to the local driving range with as much aloofness as I could muster. The day finally came one late summer afternoon when Sam was around three-and-a-half years old, a bit younger than when I first entered the game. Nonetheless, I figured the younger the better. Besides, my wife had dramatically announced "it was time."

Once at the range, I unceremoniously handed him his new U.S. Kid's Club and simply told him to hit the ball. He looked at me with large curious eyes. Wanting to be as non-intrusive and passive as possible, I simply waved him off with my hand and told him to swing away. At that point, I picked up my own club and began to do the same, hoping he would get the idea from watching me.

After a few minutes, I glanced up and discovered to my surprise Sam flailing away like a left hander. I smiled in the all-knowing way we fathers tend to master when we raise young children. I walked over, uncrossed his hands, placed them in the right-sided position, and turned him around. I then felt confident that he would now blast away, given the fact that he was already swinging a tennis racket and a bat right handed, not to mention the fact that he was coloring and scribbling (amid subtle references to Picasso uttered between my wife and me) with the right hand as well. I recall that he was even throwing a ball right handed. However, the next time I looked up, he was swinging from the "wrong side" again.

At this point, like a good father should, I became impatient. But something halted my next step. Instead, I providentially thought of Phil Mickelson, who swings from the left side, and decided to let Sam swing away. To be like the number two money winner on the PGA Tour could not be a bad idea after all. Later on, I would uncover more of Phil's story and realize the importance of this decision.

The next day, I found a left handed club for Sam at the local golf shop, and he has been swinging left handed ever since. An otherwise right handed boy, he is now going on seven years old and still swinging paradoxically from the left side. He frequently hits the ball in the air and straight away some 75 to 100 yards. The amazing part of his game, however, is not just his driving, but his chipping and putting. His control is excellent, and while I have no delusions of him becoming a prodigy pro golfer akin to Tiger (not yet anyway), I firmly believe he is destined to avoid the struggle between the dominant and non-dominant hemispheres. Why? Simply because as a left handed golfer, his dominant side is toward the target, thus avoiding the frustration of most of us right handers.

I still knew that for those of us right handers who learned golf at a later age, the odds of switching the dominant side toward the target were virtually zero to none. I also realized that the window for making this strategic move likely narrowed around three to four years of age as the brain nerve cells began to insulate and finalize the dominant pathways determining handedness. As we have said, however, left handers might be more likely to have mixed dominance and make this change more easily than their right handed counterparts.

Ability, Availability, Affability and Adaptability

As I continued to take Sam to the range, I grew more and more interested in his rather natural... (I swear)... interest in golf and decided to invest in golf lessons for him. This turned out to be a good move for Sam as well as for me. His teacher was creative and made lessons fun. It doesn't take a neurologist to know the absence of a child's attention leads to boredom and eventual chaos. I think a student's failure to learn a lesson can be just as much the fault of the teacher as the student. Call me bitter, but I have to recall that one instructor who didn't realize my swing was in fact being completed at the point of contact with the ball rather than being "unfinished." But more about this later.

This gentleman, however, was a true teacher. He practiced the four A's of any successful teacher: ability, availability, affability and adaptability. I usually placed myself near the two and would occupy my time hitting balls with a five or six iron. Whenever Sam took a break before another segment of his lesson, Sam's teacher would glance over to my direction and study my excuse for a swing. Over the next several weeks, he began to make a well-placed suggestion or two with vivid images in a Harvey Penickish sort of way. (I later learned that when the instructor was a college golfer, he used to drive to Austin on weekends to take a lesson from "The Great One.")

With no lesson scheduled and a free day ahead of us, one weekend the family and I decided to drive to Dallas so my wife could enjoy some shopping for the kids. As we exited the freeway, a surrealistic scene that I remembered from my boyhood appeared before us. Six Flags Over Texas, the coup d'etat of amusement parks in the South. Suddenly, the passengers in my car bubbled with excitement. "Could we?! Can we?! C'mon Dad!" The next thing I knew, we were standing in line for rides in the middle of the park.

For me, it brought back old memories. But more importantly, that day I saw something that would change my perception of golf forever.

Chapter Five

The Golf Gods Speak

A ride like none other appeared around the next corner. It was so unique that I almost doubted it was real. For starters, this ride had room for only two people. This was not a ride with cars or with boats. Rather, two people were covered by what appeared to be two pieces of foam rubber, and they were lashed side by side like two weenies in a hotdog bun. (Fortunately, I captured the image on film—see for yourself in the Appendix.)

They were then hoisted up to the roof of a "house," barely able to walk with their legs sticking out of this foam sandwich. Once on the roof, they were attached by a hook to a long steel cord whose origin was at the top of a tower.

Amazingly, they were then laid horizontally, and they began to be slowly ratcheted upward for what seemed like hundreds of feet. I recalled the ominous name of this ride—*Dead Man's Alley*—and shuddered. Upon reaching the zenith, the ant-like people below waited in great anticipation to see what would happen next. The next moment was simply spectacular.

Suddenly, the dynamic duo released themselves from the snare that bound them, with one brave rider's pull on a rip-cord device. Thus began the free fall, suspended by the steady cable. I instinctively began to scan the immediate area to ensure these two Orville and Wilburish kids were not on a collision course with an unforgiving wall. I breathed a sigh of relief when I realized all was clear.

Two forces guided their flight—the gravitational pull and the centripetal force countered by the one attached cord high above them. The stored potential energy now released in milliseconds resulted in an almost perfect flight over the heads of amazed park patrons below.

I smiled. I laughed. I felt great. My wife, amazed at my outburst, asked if I wanted to ride.

"No," I said emphatically. But the scene stayed with me for some time after that.

I could not shake this picture worth a thousand words, and it had a profound effect on me for what was then an unknown reason. I realize those of us in the medical profession can be known for seeing things "differently" and developing an acute appreciation for the unusual. (How many people do you know who keep Gray's Anatomy on their reading list?) But this was unusual even for me, and I don't hesitate to liken it to a metaphysical experience.

I had had the beginnings of a revelation.

An Unusual Request

It all came together for me at a break at a golf lesson for Sam. As I hit ball after ball, Sam's instructor, eyeing my swing, made an unusual request. He suggested that I swing utilizing only the left arm. This meant that I would be swinging with my dominant right arm totally off of the club. He asked me to pick out a wedge, tee up the ball and practice with a full swing (see the Appendix for an illustration).

That singular suggestion became my task for the next month. As I began to swing, it was very awkward. When I asked him to demonstrate how he did it, I was amazed. He took the club back using only the left hand, swung downward and through and produced a wonderful ball flight. My own results were less astonishing.

But I practiced harder. I continued to sacrifice balls from each practice bucket. With time, I began to strike the ball more effectively. At the finish, I found my body facing to the target with my left arm above my head and shoulder while holding onto the club…and through it all, seemingly expending no effort.

The fact is, it just happened. And I felt great.

The vivid image of the release of potential energy at Six Flags flashed before me, except now it was a picture of the release of the golf club. I realized this exercise produced a pure release of stored potential energy generated from the golf swing itself, utilizing the non-dominant side of the brain and the left side of the body. Like the period of disconnection similar to the patients in my epilepsy study, the right brain was suddenly "cut loose" and released from what was "binding" it. This was the right side of the brain in all its glory—taking the wheel of the left side of the body and doing its own thing. I realized for the first time the simple benefit of the left side of the golf swing:

It felt absolutely correct…even though I had no idea how I did it at the time.

Disconnection Drill

I came to realize that the more I hit with the left arm alone, the more I encountered the "feel-good feeling" we talked about earlier. I was tapping into the right side of the brain's center of pleasure with this "disconnection drill." Remember reading about my patients with strokes involving the right side of the brain who appear saddened, morose, depressed and incapable of showing any emotion? Have you ever returned from the course feeling somewhat like that? I know I have. I've had days where I haven't even come close to tapping into the right side. But the cycle of pleasure and consistency, more pleasure and more consistency that came from utilizing the right side of my brain was so motivating. I was anxious to see what I could do next.

Disconnection Drill Pointers

*This drill is the closest thing to isolating
the non-dominant side of the brain
Be aware of the feel when you catch
the ball with a full left arm swing
When done correctly, there should be a
release of potential energy from the golf swing
Use a lofted club like a wedge
(not a driver), and even tee it up
What about the right hand? Honestly,
I'm not sure what I do with mine during the swing.
Perhaps that is the way it should be!
My son's teacher plays a round of golf occasionally with
his students using only the left arm on the club.
Usually, he beats them all. So, it can be done!*

Perfect Harmony

Continuing to take my son to lessons, I awaited another tip from the teacher. I knew I could not continue to hit with the left hand only. At some point, I had to place the right hand back on the club. One day, while hitting particularly thin shots, the window of opportunity opened. During one of Sam's breaks, the instructor suggested I try a new drill. He asked me to swing the club, stopping it out in front of me with arms extended. I recalled a similar picture of Tiger in that position in the swing and felt immediately oriented to the image. I gave it a try.

When I stopped the club, however, my wrists were already released, with my right hand pushing the club upward. No deal. I was unable to come within 90 degrees of extension. My right hand, taking orders from the left side of the brain, was completely dominating the entire drill. No extension. No rotation of the hands. Most importantly, no feeling of participation from the left side of the body. The right side of the brain had gone AWOL, figuring it would never be missed, and dominance ruled my swing!

The ball flight was compromised by a thin hit as a result of topping. This also was the result of the breakdown of the swing and the dominance of the right hand/left brain at impact. It dawned on me that this was the very aspect of my swing that had caused my former teaching pro to inform me that I was not completing my swing. Of course, the swing was being completed! The problem was that the dominant left side of the brain declared the swing complete at impact, thus resulting in a tendency to lift the head and eyes to track the ball's flight. This is what I had been doing for years. How relieved I was to discover that it was not psychological but neurological.

Translation? It was a brain thing!

In response, I began to practice swinging the club to try to get the arms extended and the wrists rotating together. (See the Appendix to get a better idea of what this should look like). I did this second and newest swing exercise almost exclusively for a month. I would stop the club shortly past impact, making sure rotation occurred with good extension of the forearms and arms. Coupled with moving the right foot upward and a feel for the shoulders in the proper position, I began to understand how I could hit the ball with more power and without my lifelong slice. Harvey Penick comments that the wrists play little role in the swing, but rotating the forearms provides the "punch in the shot." [2]

With time, I began to understand the swing a little better with this harmonizing technique. The palm surface of each forearm must approximate the other through impact. However, this is also the portion of the swing where many right handed amateurs may not have been able to deliver because it forces the hands to work together. My goal became finding exercises or swing techniques that forced the hands, therefore the brain halves, to work equally.

Harmonizing Drill Pointers

During the course of the downswing,
one must rotate the forearms in harmony
This is the point of great power
Practice this drill often. In fact,
it can be very effective if one uses the swing thought
of finishing with forearms approximating each other.
The rotational release through impact is even more
effective if one can learn to keep the head still
and a little more behind the ball at impact
I have always been told that when you see a player
rotating his arms effectively through the golf swing,
don't play him for money. But do play him to
observe first hand what he does in his swing.

Attention Golfers: Do Not Replace Divots

On still another occasion, the instructor gave me a third exercise to do. This, too, was a harmonizing drill. I simply call it the "divot drill" and liken it to Harvey Penick's gimmick drill utilizing a weed cutter. One cannot cut heavy weeds (the kind that grow down here in Texas), without a strong, straight left hand, arm and wrist. Likewise, the divot drill requires a straightened left arm and wrist at impact to even get the balls out! The divot drill is a surefire way of demonstrating what the stiff left wrist is all about and is best utilized, by the way, in the rugged, unforgiving Bermuda grass of my home state where only a correct swing will extricate the ball. (While you're visiting, you might want to make a run to Six Flags Over Texas and see the marvelous demonstration of the release of potential energy that so influenced my perception of the swing.) I use a five or six iron and align the divot somewhat in the middle in my stance. At the end of this repetitive drill, the divot is oftentimes ten to twelve inches long—a sure sign that the club is staying in the "groove" longer.

As I spent more time with the third phase of my exercise trinity,

I further realized the advantage of utilizing the left arm controlled by the non-dominant right side of the brain in good swing technique. It somehow promoted movement upward of the right foot quickly in the downswing, as though this was intuitively necessary to get the ball out and on its way. Still, another positive aspect of this drill was the fact that one tended to maintain focus on the divot longer. In contrast, a lack of participation by the left side of the body leads to a tendency to "look up" as one makes contact with the ball. Result? A thin hit, topping the ball. However, the divot drill decreases the tendency to lift the head and come out of the swing too soon at impact and gives the added bonus of keeping the head still and behind the ball at impact.

I even know a golfer who asked his fellow players to let him hit out of a divot. That was the way he hit the ball correctly on every shot. Need I even tell you that his testimony to me was one of enjoying the great pleasure that this produced?

Divot Drill Pointers

*This requires a straightened left arm
and wrist at impact to even get the balls out!
Keep your head down, still and behind the ball at impact
Realize the role the left side of the body
plays in good swing technique
This drill can be done anytime, anywhere divots can be
found. Do not be fooled by ads offering to
send you a box of divots for $19.95.
Like many aspects of my recommendations in this book,
divots are free.*

Now, We're Cooking

As I continued with these drills, I began to actually feel for the first time the consistency of the left side of the body in the swing. I believe golfing more from the right side of the brain allowed me to activate and feel an emotional reward in my harmonizing drills.

That pleasurable experience alone is worth the cost of the book and a day at the range trying out golfing from the right side of the brain.

Allowing the right side of the brain to participate in the swing furthermore seemed to have a sustaining effect on my practice sessions, unlike previous times at the range. I also continued to hit balls with the left arm only to keep in touch with the right side of the brain function even more.

The key word here is "harmony." Attempts to suppress the dominant side of the body will only meet with frustration. Similarly, trying to simply "relax" the right side of the body or willfully trying to avoid allowing it to participate in the swing leads to even more intrusion. Ready for a shocker? The use of devices or exercises to modify the position of the right hand, arm and body do little to modify brain dominance. Remember, it's a brain thing you're up against! Not to mention the fact that these devices are illegal in play during an actual round of golf. What's a body to do once these devices come off? Well, it usually reverts to a quick return to the old swing.

In contrast, with my new set of swing exercises and techniques, my swing became simpler and significantly more compact. Coupled with my three exercises mentioned above, I tried to incorporate a sound and standard grip that basically tips the left hand grip a little more into the palm and the right hand a little more into the fingers. I have also practiced a waggle à la Ben Hogan, which I have used in my setup and to start my swing. I have sought to keep my left arm straighter on the back swing and to initiate my downswing by allowing my right foot to come up. The result? A release of the club along a predictable swing path. Of course, I have also tried to finish with good forearm rotation and with arms extended.

What can I say? I consider my journey to golfing from the right side of the brain to have begun with these very techniques—and I encourage you to begin your own journey here as well. Although I initially focused on each drill for about a month, I consider these to be lifetime drills. I continue to use these drills as a warm up to my round and find myself practicing rotating my wrists together even during my game.

I feel the disconnection and harmonizing drills outlined in this book give the reader new hope and may put her or him on the right track toward a more complete swing. Best of all, they don't cost a thing! The only resources you need are a ball and a club. They may not change your life, but they'll bring new life into your swing.

Chapter Six

Gimmicks, Hi-Tech and Video Tapes

S o why is it so hard to have an effective golf swing anyway? Well, if you understand that golf is a brain game, it may not be that difficult. And I don't think we all should hire a sports neurologist or psychologist to help us. I believe nervousness and anxiety over the swing occur because of disappointment, resulting from the fact that most of us do not experience the expected results that the non-dominant side of the brain can produce. For example, a sensation of pleasure bordering on euphoria comes when one experiences an awareness of the left side of the body. And I believe this experience can and will come.

But how did golf evolve to this point of the haves and the have-nots? As I've said, most people (with rare exception) hit from the outside in when they swing. Surely such a great game should not produce such a dichotomy in the ability of its participants. With the plethora of technological and instructional aids today, why don't we have the capability of solving the problem?

In this country, we tend to buy more videos and golf instructional books than anyone else in the world. We sit and listen to our teachers tell us about ten steps to a better swing. In turn, those ten steps generally involve just as many tedious positions for a cumulative swing of less than a second. Videos sell by the thousands every year, giving one a mental picture of what the perfect swing should be like. The more verbal left side of the brain, of course, takes all of this in with great interest. And yet, beyond being a recipient of more verbiage, the simple fact is nothing changes. Can't our professional teaching pros, physicists, sports psychologists and equipment manufacturers come up with a suitable answer to correct this glaring inconsistency in the swing? They can, if they understand it's a brain thing.

Perhaps the answer lies in a novel approach such as I have proposed in this very book. The benefits include using simple drills that allow a golfer to self-manage his or her progress and produce results. The idea of no money down and no monthly payments should also be appealing to most. The fact that these drills minimize the verbiage-intensity the left brain loves and are directed instead to the non-dominant right side of the brain should convince even the most frustrated duffer to try it. I believe the right side of the brain has suffered from neglect long enough.

Perhaps this approach may even generate more practical research by influential scientists, supported by the golf industry. And maybe even our neurologists and neurophysiologists will have something to say as well. It is a brain thing, you know.

Yikes! It's the Yips

Already, neurologists are seeing golfers about a certain kind of process called dystonia. Dystonia is a brain condition that results in uncontrollable motor activity in the body or certain parts of the body. It may involve simply an extremity, like hands, or the whole body itself. These are unwanted, uncontrollable movements that come at the worst time. Golfers recognize it as a condition called the "yips." In the practice of neurology, we may see it as part of a degenerative condition or from medication effects on the brain. The bottom line is that this condition is most definitely a brain thing.

The general scenario involves a loss of fine motor control, most commonly as one stands over the ball to putt. Articles are now appearing, even in our professional neurological journals, regarding this malady. I suspect and hope that neurologists may offer some benefit in regards to this career-ending abnormality. Unlike the yips, there is no medicine or psychotherapy that will help one golf from the right side of the brain. It is not a disease process combated with medicine or surgery. It simply requires mostly an awareness of its existence and an application of specific principles and exercise.

But why reserve neurology to speak only to maladies? It's not that I wish to be considered for the PGA as a sports neurologist, nor am I campaigning for the position of Father of Sports Neurology, (although it does have a nice ring to it).

Rather, I strongly feel that instead of trying to uncover the latest and greatest technology or gimmick, we may have neglected long-standing knowledge we already have. About the evolution of our understanding of the brain. And about the evolution of the game itself to see if we can figure out how it became such a fascinating challenge for most of us. These are strictly my thoughts and extrapolations, mind you, and in no way imply that I am an expert about golf history. But if you're still reading this, you've hung with my theories thus far, so see what you think about these ideas.

Whip It

Golf is said to have originated in Great Britain, of course, with the Scots. The courses were carved out of land between the ocean and civilization. The "links" were grassy, windy and tests of great skill. The shafts of the original clubs used were carved from wooden branches. The balls were less than substantial but functional. The wooden shafts were flexible, and the swing began with a great sweep wide and to the right. As the golfer turned his body, he sought to get the club high in the air. Next came a release with a great turn to the left.

As the club began its decent, the player did something I imagine was necessitated solely by the flexible shaft. He stiffened up the left leg and hip and brought the lower body to somewhat of a halt. The next step was to wait as the club "whipped" its way to the ball. The result was a great acceleration of the club for quite a distance along the now committed swing path. Voila! The advent of the golf swing.

Ironically, this basic process continued until the 1930s with the production of the steel shaft. At this point, Byron Nelson stepped up with new ideas to accommodate the more predictable but less flexible "steel sticks." He began to advocate utilizing the left side of the body more which resulted in the more modern swing in today's game. This innovation may have evolved from a need to generate greater swing speed, seemingly lost with the passing of the once popular whippy shafts.

This was the beginning of the new era of golf. While most professionals at the time became comfortable with the transition, a few continued to advocate more right-sided forces in the swing, and some even continued to use the wooden sticks. Tommy Armour, "The Flying Scot," actually advocated the idea that many right handed golfers would benefit from the increased use of the right side, given it was controlled by the more dominant left side of the brain.[3]

In the end, however, the modern swing and steel shafts won out. Perhaps the very difficulty amateurs have with the swing came to fruition at this time. With the elimination of variation in feel from club to club came an equally difficult problem. Most modern day amateur golfers unknowingly struggled with surrendering some of the input from the right side of the body in the form of less whippy shafts. Likewise, the ability to incorporate more left-sided function may have been too much to ask. The very lack of "skill" required to bring into harmony the two sides of the body may, in fact, have resulted in the great prevalence of the now classic out-to-in swing flaw.

Ben Hogan attempted to explain the fundamental aspects of the modern swing in a brilliant, albeit complexly written and illustrated book.[4] His use of the waggle, emphasis on the straight left arm and drawings of the correct grip were extremely important to understanding the new golf swing.

Isn't it ironic that this gentleman was left handed, but his swing was from the right side? Sound familiar? Hogan, perhaps the greatest teacher of the swing, was also able to demonstrate time after time the way it was supposed to be done. However, he had the dominant side to the target.

I suspect the brain dynamics in Hogan's swing were likewise

different from the vast majority of players, both professional and amateur. Perhaps there is something novel about being left handed, given the fact that mixed language and motor dominance are far greater in the left handers. The fact is, the incidence of language being paired with handedness is about as frequent as a coin toss or fifty-fifty. All pointing to a far different brain than right handers who are likely to have 96% dominance/language association.

Next on the Horizon

The next significant change in equipment began in the late 80s and early 90s, the beginning of the graphite shaft era. However, for a brief time, some of you may recall that fiberglass shafts led the way. Of interest was the fact that these clubs were whippy and so unmanageable in the average golfer's swing that they quickly gave way to graphite, a far more rigid material than fiberglass. Graphite, of course, became a major material for drivers and fairway woods.

In retrospect, the fiberglass shafts were perhaps introduced in an attempt to restore the earlier more flexible clubs (and create a lighter weight club that could be matched as a set). Unfortunately, the instructions about the original swing (stiffening the left-sided impact, etc.) did not find their way into the new era. I suspect they were packed away with grandpa's monocle, knickers and three piece suits—irrelevant pieces of history. The amazing thing is that graphite shafts stayed around anyway, likely because they were so lightweight.

In the modern era of golf, the ongoing search for the clubs and balls that will improve the game continues. Imagination and technology may even cause some changes radical enough to allow major adjustments in the swing again. However, for now and in the future, I believe golf will remain a brain thing resulting in growing interest in golfing from the right side of the brain, regardless of which shaft one chooses to use.

Chapter Seven

Neuro-Circuitry 101

If you remember, I promised you that fascinating neuro-circuitry lecture earlier on in my introduction. Well, the wait is finally over. Introducing, adaptability and afferent input. Now, that's a mouthful. Webster's defines adaptability as: *the ability to be able to change without difficulty so as to conform to new or changed circumstances.* Let me see if I can put it into English.

Basically, any new information or "afferent" (input to the brain) changes regarding a previously learned task (such as a golf swing) results in a certain amount of brain processing to accommodate this new afferent data. Hopefully, this processing produces great results. (Recall the "successful" adjustments Byron Nelson introduced with the advent of steel shafts.) In fact, this process is what the makers of golf equipment and technology are banking on. And it works...at least for a while. The rush to buy the latest technology is not entirely off-base. Even when a new product is introduced to the average player and his or her brain, it results in an intense new input that allows the golfer to actually "feel" the club. This attention to new afferent detail likely is the very cause of the so-called honeymoon phase, which leads to all sorts of endorsements in the office and at the country club. Unfortunately, this new stuff becomes old stuff after a few weeks, and the old swing or lack thereof remains.

(See the Appendix for a shameless personal photo of this axiom).

Muscle Memory Class Cancelled

A related topic is the idea of muscle-memory. People often talk to me about the term, "muscle memory." The concept seems to be that repetition in practice somehow results in information being stored up for future use. There is some truth to this, but the term itself is a bit simplistic and tends to avoid giving credit where credit is due. This process is a brain thing, of course.

I want to remind you at this point that the brain has the ability to process information received from the various parts of the body including joints, skin, deep tissues and muscle. From here, this "afferent information" is stored as memory in the brain for future use depending on perceived importance and consistency of repetition. You may be surprised, however, to learn that the degree of benefit and the end result (adaptability) may depend not just on repetition, but rather the *kind* of input the brain is asked to process.

Neurologically speaking, you're already somewhat familiar with the idea of adaptability from what you read in a previous chapter regarding my epilepsy surgery fellowship. Recall the patient who had his brain surgically disconnected and the extended time it took his brain to adapt. For many months he could not even function. However, due to the brain's ability to adapt to new situations, this patient was able to eventually enjoy a relatively good quality of life, with far fewer severe, frequent seizures resulting from the deep brain connections that had made the surgery necessary in the first place.

Likewise, in the process of a single golf lesson or round of golf, the brain tests new connections and processes data coming from a variety of sensors in the joints, on the skin and deeper within the tissues. Pressure, velocity and position for each aspect of the swing are recorded and must be incorporated. More data from our special sense organs such as the eyes and ears are also analyzed. This data makes its way to the deeper parts of the brain and spreads upward to the white and gray matter, where processing begins. While you're out enjoying a gentle breeze on a summer afternoon, eyeing the fairway, the brain is in fact very busy. In fact, we are rarely aware or conscious of the entire goings on inside our brains. (Who says golf is a mindless hobby anyway?)

Besides this "intrinsic activity," the golfer is also subjected to a myriad of external factors in the environment that may interfere with the ability to make the shot. Unlike more commonly played sports of baseball, football, basketball and tennis, golf does not have a uniform, defined playing field. For example, if one were to travel to most any country in the world to play baseball, one would have the same reasonable expectations for play, placement of the baselines, an infield and outfield, etc.

However, the golf course contains undulating terrain that varies from course to course and from hole to hole. No matter the location, one is destined to meet with unpredictables such as wind, water, sand, fast greens, wet greens, sloping greens, heavy rough, mighty trees, dog-legs, and/or long par fours. What a challenge! It's why I love this game! But the remaining question is: How does one deal with the greatest of all challenges—maintaining a consistent swing amid all the variable afferent input?

Consistency Is Key

Ben Hogan somehow incorporated a great deal of consistency whenever possible. An avid practitioner, he did this by taking extensive notes during his practice sessions. He never advocated trying to change anything regarding the swing during a round of golf. He knew somehow that to put the least "afferent" demand on the brain created less stress and need for adaptability, resulting in more reliability and consistency in the swing.

Of course, Ben Hogan may very well be different from you the reader, given the fact that golf was both his vocation and avocation. In his later years, he certainly had more time to pursue the perfection of the swing. In his aforementioned book, he produced a masterpiece of instruction complete with text and drawings.

Yet who is in such a similar position today to spend many hours changing or perfecting our swing? For the avid but average players, decisions have to be made as to how to manage and approach our own golf practice. Unless you have the personality, time and motivational traits that belong to professional golfers, especially one like Ben Hogan, then you must take matters into your own hands and devise a program that suits your needs. Along with this proactive attitude, you must have a teacher and a plan which fit your busy schedule and lifestyle. In other words, try to get the best lesson for your time and money. However, as Harvey Penick once said, "Lessons are not to take the place of practice but to make practice worthwhile." [5]

Nobody likes to change, including your brain. Given the fact that adaptability is a very complex process, as we've noted, I have come up with a few guidelines to streamline the endeavor.

- **Small change, big difference** – Be aware that even small, individual changes that you and your pro decide to make may certainly have an extensive effect on the overall swing. Paraphrasing Penick, he reminds us that if he changed a player's grip, the player returning for a second lesson would have a whole different swing.

- **Change takes time** – Realize that the more changes you are subjected to during a teaching session, the longer the brain will take to adapt to each change proposed. The brain must have enough reinforcement through your practice sessions with selective and effective practice techniques. "If I ask you to take one aspirin, don't take the whole bottle." [6]

- **Develop a pre-shot routine** – By doing this, you alert the brain with a consistent afferent input frequently resulting in successful shot-making. In this regard, I think most teaching professionals would agree, "it's a brain thing." Remember, the more consistent the afferent information is regarding your swing, the less demand you place on the brain during an actual round of golf.

- **Less talk. More action.** – Be aware of the possibility that too much verbal input during the instruction period may make the desired brain adaptation more difficult. Remember the "telephone" game when you were a kid? By the time the information wafted down the line to your ears, the original message was usually muddled. Similarly, language is processed in the left side of the brain and transferred secondhand to the right side of the brain. What the right side of the brain is more attuned to is feel, spatial concepts and overall body position. The more direct "right brain" drills discussed in this book should result in a greater awareness of the left side of the body. At that point, you're "speaking" the right brain's language. Watch your teacher with other students and observe how he or she varies the lessons. Watch to see if the teacher spends more time correcting students' swings with hands on or by observing and occasionally interrupting with a well-timed suggestion. In my opinion, the less verbiage used, the more effective the teacher.

- **This is a job for a professional** – I can assure you that having a professional who is at least familiar with the drills that promote more direct input to the right brain will be a great advantage. In exchange, you will enjoy an awareness and insight that can only be the product of the holistic and non-dominant right brain. Ask your teacher to tell you why you slice the ball if and when you do. Ask if the teacher has had much success in curing a slice rather than patching it up. If your teacher has had little success in curing a slice, you might consider moving on. Give him or her your respect for the honesty. It's a hard thing for any teaching pro to admit.

I hope that these suggestions are beneficial if you would like to try golfing from the right side of the brain. My belief is that following these guidelines may lead to a more efficient and pleasurable swing. Practice the three exercises hard, and I suspect that your game will at least improve, if not significantly so.

Chapter Eight

A Trip to the Bookstore

As I began writing this book, I paid a trip to the local Barnes & Noble Bookstore. I was particularly interested in the golf section and who was writing golf books. "Perhaps there were other physicians who had the same interest in this great sport," I thought to myself. After all, we've already mentioned how the "yips" have become a recognized neurological problem, and many professional players are seeking help for this problem today.

To my surprise, I found only one book written by a psychiatrist and a few by psychologists. These books talked at length about the psychological aspects of the game, including various manifestations of anxiety and even negativity from which golfers suffer. Depression also made its way into several chapters.

I became very interested in these books as I realized that my book might benefit those with various disorders of the psyche since golfing from the right side of the brain has been a source of pleasurable experiences for me and many who have tried it. Golfers who are in touch with the pleasure and emotional centers unique to the right side of the brain are in touch with greater enjoyment of the game as well. The idea of a more accurate swing making the game more enjoyable makes sense from a practical and medical standpoint.

Glancing up and down shelf after shelf of golfing books, I

realized how many different kinds of people are writing golf books today. Touring professionals. Teaching professionals. Sports psychologists. I was surprised to even see the American novelist, John Updike, had written on the subject. The author list continued with physicists and even publishers in the familiar Dummies category.

However, a book on the *Five Fundamentals of Hogan*[7] caught my eye. I settled down in an overstuffed chair, Starbucks in hand, and flipped through the pages of this extensive treatise on the Hogan grip and swing. One page of the book got my attention right away. It was a photograph of Hogan performing a unique exercise Hogan said he particularly enjoyed. In the picture, he was hitting balls swinging the club with the right arm alone. In the caption below the picture was a subtle reference to the fact that Hogan was a natural left hander, swinging from the right side.

I mechanically put down my cup without lifting my eyes from the page as I continued to read with great interest.

The author pointed out that this exercise was particularly special to Hogan because it allowed him to "feel the non-dominant" right side alone in the swing. Aha! No wonder it was said to have been a favorite and pleasurable exercise for Hogan. The key exercise I have advocated for "disconnecting" my non-dominant right side of the brain by swinging with the left arm alone was the very exercise Hogan was doing as a lefty, swinging from the right side.

If you haven't guessed by now, I am and will always be a fan of Harvey Penick. He intuitively understood the importance of the brain in the game and advocated exercises that attended to the non-dominant side of the brain as well. I sense he had an understanding of the harmony of the swing and realized its importance in producing an effective swing. I suspect it also gave him that sense of pleasure that earned him the reputation of being a "contented" man. *The Little Red Book*[8] is one of my favorite publications of all time. After finishing off my java and reshelving the Hogan book, I hurried home to review Penick's writings, fueled by this new information (and perhaps the double shot of espresso). The result was even more confirmation that I was on the right track with my theories.

Please, Check All Books at the Clubhouse

I had begun to suspect the weed cutter exercise I described earlier, similar to the divot drill, was an attempt on Penick's part to harmonize the two hemispheres of the brain. And, in fact, Penick's book emphasizes the same essentials outlined in my three disconnection drills and harmonization exercises. For example, Penick advocated keeping the head still and behind the ball through impact.

Reminiscent of my Six Flags revelation, Penick also pointed out that when one is swinging correctly, a natural release will occur...such as the one I had experienced earlier in my drill. Given the fact that confidence in the swing occurs only when one *has* a swing, it is essential to feel that rotation of the arms and release as soon as possible. I have found that swinging with a conscious effort to rotate the forearms through the swing so the palm side of each forearm comes to approximate the other through impact will begin to give almost instant "afferent" feedback and result in a natural release. Perhaps for many of us who do not have that excellent swing, the next best thing would be to concentrate as much as possible on allowing that release to happen through the swing thought of approximating the forearms through the ball.

One will soon come to realize the power and distance that can be had with this drill as Penick so clearly did. Remember Penick's point about the rotation of the forearms providing the punch in the shot? Even as one ages, this is one part of the swing that keeps your game intact. I also suggest that you actually take this rotation exercise out to the course and use it in your round, especially if things are going awry. Stopping the swing with both arms in extension on the follow-through will result in instant feedback as to the correctness of the swing at that point. (Incidentally, who is going to laugh at you when they see the ball flight resulting form this abbreviated swing? You have nothing to lose.)

Many people wonder why they can swing well with the few practice "swishes" they perform in preparation for their tee shot and then are unable to deliver with the shot itself. A return to the *Little Red Book* partially clarifies this for us. Penick attributed this to an intrusion of thought to consciously square up the club with the real swing. However, perhaps a conscious effort to rotate the arms through impact (by attempting to approximate the forearms) will likely result in a more reasonable result, thus overriding a subconscious "intrusion" to square up the club face. This seems to work for me.

Golf: Meant to Be a Happy Game

Take a trip to the bookstore yourself. Look at Ben Hogan's book, especially the section on the grip and discussion about the waggle. Strive to keep the head still and behind the ball through impact like both Harvey Penick and Ben Hogan suggested. Lastly, when you need some help, I want to suggest again that you see your teaching pro. Penick relates that a good teacher can reveal in one hour what ordinarily would take one six months to figure out. The bottom line, he also notes, is getting a system of some kind. Any kind of system beats sheer luck. Finally, be patient. With time and appropriate attention to other aspects of the game, you will find a greater degree of satisfaction with your practice.

For me, the orientation of golf to the brain is a logical one. I'll admit I have some advantage, being a practicing neurologist and all. However, I feel these suggestions have a logical basis in golf which anyone can understand. As I said before, don't go looking for a sports neurologist to help your game (unless you really do have the yips). Remember, golf is meant to be a happy game (spoken from a man who once doubted the truthfulness of that statement). Seek out those people who seem to enjoy the game as a result of the swing. Watch them and see what they do. You may see some of these tips being demonstrated in their swings.

Chapter Nine

Unsolved Mysteries

Of course, I realize that these observations will likely be just that for now and nothing more. Perhaps you picked this book up at the airport bookstore and it's seen you through the end of your flight without any benefit as far as your golf game is concerned. However, before you return your tray table to the upright and locked position and start listening for gate information, stay with me for one more moment, if you will. I may actually need *your* input at this point.

You see, I have a few final observations involving people who bring unique characteristics into the mix. One, as I mentioned, is my father, who taught me to play the game. He is left handed, but swings comfortably right handed. I find this fascinating but reasonably explained by mixed dominance that commonly exists in left handers. Nonetheless, I can't help but wonder if my dad was doing it "right" because he somehow felt that the dominant left side seemed correct all along when placed toward the target.

Perhaps Ben Hogan knew the same thing when he chose to swing right handed. Somehow this man went beyond all expectations in grip control and ability to swing the club accurately and consistently. Hogan definitely fits in the category of unique golfers.

I would like to ask Nick Price and Johnny Miller the same questions about their natural left handedness. In fact, I would like to get a list of tour professionals who are left handed but swing right. But they'd probably have to shoot me afterwards for uncovering this information.

Sam also defies the expected as a right hander who swings from the left. (Of course, his photo is proudly placed in the Appendix.) I serendipitously learned Phil Mickelson started hitting balls at eighteen months of age, swinging from the left side. Yet he was otherwise a natural right hander. I suspect that age indeed was a factor in determining which side was preferentially placed toward the target. In other words, Phil's brain was not yet restricted to completed dominance. Likewise, Phil's father had his toddler son mirroring his own right handed swing—putting Phil in the left handed position facing his father. Perhaps Sam's experience was not so different given his first lesson was at such a young age, coupled with his attempt to face me and "do what I do." Given the fact that this phenomenon seems to be rare indeed (and that my son continues to swing left handed), one can only scratch one's head and wonder.

But you know the most amazing paradox of all is the experience of Earl Woods with his son, Tiger.[9] At six months to one year of age, Tiger watched his dad swing right handed while Tiger was merely a cub sitting in a high chair. At one year of age, Tiger began to hit balls "left handed" into a net with apparently greater-than-expected skill. Could this have been another "pre-dominance phenomenon" caused by the mirroring of his dad's right handed swing? Of course, the answer remains uncertain since Tiger, unlike my son Sam, spontaneously changed his swing to right handed two weeks into this experience without Earl's prodding. And the rest is history. While Earl Woods states that Tiger was left handed, it is unclear whether this was actually transient or not. Nonetheless, it is remarkable stuff and gives rise to more questions than answers.

From my own point of view, I am glad I didn't keep turning my son around that day. To do so in a kid showing even right handed tendencies, it still could have been confusing…despite the fact that there is less leeway in mixed dominance in right handers than in left.

Five-and-a-Half Inch Course

Of course, I still think back to the time when my wife brought home her textbook from drawing class. It truly motivated me to apply the principal to my favorite past-time as I began working to answer some questions about why the game was so difficult for the average player. I thought, in my case, it might be due to the fact that I had failed to spend enough time and money on the game. However, this cost me a lot of wasted money on foolish purchases. It almost cost me my family.

Another thought was that perhaps the golf courses had become unreasonable as far as their design. Fairways seemed impossibly narrow and the trees had somehow grown much taller. While equipment had improved, the length of the individual holes had increased and the greens were heavily bunkered, elevated and closely surrounded by rough. Gone were the days of being able to run a golf ball up to the green and let it nestle itself close to the hole as I had once done.

I began to muse that the game itself was so unreasonable that maybe it was a joke on all of us. I formulated diatribes in my mind concerning mere mortals' inability to manage the modern swing. Maybe the whole approach to the correct address was the problem. I wondered if these "natural golf" guys were really on to something after all. However, as I looked for affirmation on this theory, I didn't see these people winning the local club tournaments. I didn't see them at all. Perhaps the truth was that like the World Wrestling Federation, only professionals dared step into the ring.

Of course, now I feel that the solution may indeed lie in something as simple as *Golfing from the Right Side of the Brain*™. I think this book may indeed have answers for the average amateur to assist in understanding the modern swing. I also think it will enable him or her to become a better golfer with little in the way of expense, exhaustive hours of practice or overly detailed lessons. Coupled with what I believe should be a release of pleasure and success, I think this book will be the best answer...at least for those who wholeheartedly believe that golf is a brain thing.

> *"Competitive golf is played mainly on a five-and-a-half-inch course, the space between your ears."*
>
> *- Bobby Jones -*

Appendix

New Stuff Becomes Old Stuff

This is really not so funny, you know. My problem really surfaced out of frustration over not having a swing. This, coupled with a weakness for any sales pitch that came along, resulted in a lot of good money down the drain.

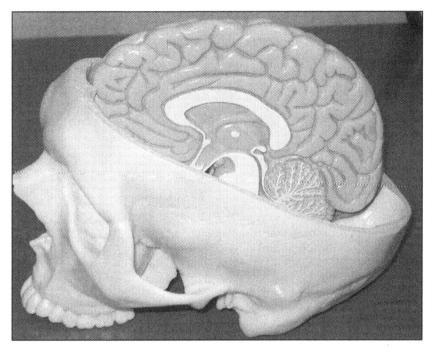

Pathways in the Brain

This model of the brain highlights the areas of connection between the two halves of the brain. These areas appear as the lighter sections of this model of the right half of the brain. These pathways allow each brain hemisphere to communicate with the other.

Surgical disconnection is occasionally done to prevent the spread of seizure activity through the pathways. This procedure results in a temporary, albeit chaotic, lack of communication between the dominant and non-dominant halves. In the end, however, the brain is somehow able to adapt and normalcy returns.

Dead Man's Alley

Like many great golf courses with a signature hole, I have deemed this photograph my signature photo. Simply put, this picture is worth a thousand words. The scene is Six Flags Over Texas, and the photograph demonstrates a great aspect of physics. The moment of release of two passengers from a point high in the sky results in the unleashing of previously stored potential energy. Little did I know at the time how much this scene would later teach me about the modern golf swing.

Disconnection Drill-Part One

The following pages contain a demonstration of one of my favorite drills. I call it the "disconnection drill" because it allows me to feel the left side of the golf swing independently of the right. In my experience, this has resulted in the ability to actually feel, for the first time, this aspect of the modern swing and to acquaint myself with golfing from the right or non-dominant side of the brain.

Disconnection Drill-Part Two

I believe this drill will allow the golfer to both sense the release of potential energy and, at the same time, experience the release of pleasure that comes with doing this drill well.

Disconnection Drill-Part Three

Ben Hogan, though left handed, likewise practiced swinging only with his non-dominant right side in order to get in touch with this aspect of the golf swing.

Harmonizing Drill

These next pictures demonstrate to me the end results of a good swing. This shot demonstrates the importance of the two harmonizing drills in my book. The first drill of intentionally approximating the forearms is evident in this photo with good release and rotation of the forearms. The good position of the head, right leg and, most importantly, the left arm and wrist, is also a result of hitting the ball out of a divot (not seen).

Also, notice where the head is positioned. It is certainly not looking to see where the ball is going. There is little doubt in my mind that solid contact was made.

Forearms Approximating

Note also that the arms are together, with forearms approximating each other and with good extension. As one can easily see, there is only harmony in the swing and a great deal of power was likely released through the ball. Note the position of the shoulders and the head in relation to the body. With this position, it is virtually impossible to come out of the swing early.

Leg, Knee, Foot Position

Last, look at the position of the right leg, knee and foot. Allowing this shift forward to come early in the downswing, permits the club to descend along the proper path and end up in a final position like we see demonstrated here.

Sam's Swing

Sam tends to do some things in his swing that I would like to be able to do in mine. I particularly like his finish, in that he likes to keep focused on the spot from where he hit the ball throughout his swing. At the same time, he keeps his head behind this same spot through impact to finish.

Allowing his back foot to come up is something he tries extra hard to do in his swing. Likewise, when he is able to approximate the forearms, he seems to enjoy the results. The main thing is that he seems to enjoy the game, and I hope he is able to avoid the frustration his father went through trying to find a swing!

Footnotes

[1] Betty Edwards, *Drawing on the Right Side of the Brain*, 2nd ed, J. P. Tarcher, 1999.

[2] Harvey Penick, *The Little Red Book: Lessons and Teachings from a Lifetime in Golf*, Simon and Schuster, 1992.

[3] For more information on the historical significance of the evolution of the swing, I have found the following especially helpful: *Golf Magazine's Complete Book of Golf Instruction*, Harry N. Abrams Publisher, 1997.

[4] Ben Hogan, Five Lessons: *The Modern Fundamentals of Golf*, Fireside Publishers, reprint edition, 1985.

[5] Harvey Penick

[6] Harvey Penick

[7] David Leadbetter, *Five Fundamentals of Hogan*, Doubleday Press, 2000.

[8] Harvey Penick

[9] Tiger Woods, *How I Play Golf*, Warner Books, NY: 2001.

CPSIA information can be obtained
at www.ICGtesting.com
Printed in the USA
BVHW071748060222
628183BV00008B/527

9 781594 672880